Successfully
Managing
Change

George Hardy

All inquiries should be addressed to:
Barron's Educational Series, Inc.
250 Wireless Boulevard
Hauppauge, New York 11788

Library of Congress Catalog Card Number 97-6357

International Standard Book No. 0-7641-0060-2

Library of Congress Cataloging-in-Publication Data
Hardy, George, 1929–
    Successfully managing change / George Hardy.
        p.   cm. — (Business success series)
    ISBN 0-7641-0060-2
    1. Organizational change—Management.   I. Title.   II. Series
HD58.8.H3643   1997
658.4'06—dc21   97-6357
                                                                CIP

PRINTED IN HONG KONG
987654321

Contents

Introduction

◆

Successful management of change is now a key issue for all organizations. Government initiatives aimed at promoting change have added to the impact of those changes that organizations inflict on themselves.

Coping with change is sometimes viewed, unnecessarily, as extremely difficult. This book provides an understanding of change to help managers cope more easily with it.

We will look at these different aspects of change:

◆ Understanding change

◆ Managing during change

◆ Strategies for managing change

◆ Resistance to change

◆ Dealing with resistance to change

◆ The psychological impact of change

◆ Introducing change

Reference in the book to *managers* implies managers at any level—directors, managers, supervisors, and foremen. Reference to *staff* implies subordinates in any capacity.

Chapter 1

Understanding Change

Let us begin by talking about understanding change and ways of coping with it. We will look at:

◆ The nature of change and a framework for understanding it

◆ Obstacles to managing change effectively

◆ Coping well with change

◆ Force field analysis and its relevance to the management of change

THE NATURE OF CHANGE AND A FRAMEWORK FOR UNDERSTANDING IT

Change is not new, otherwise we would still be using the quill pen. Two developments have affected the concept of change in recent years:

◆ Change has become constant.

◆ The pace of change has accelerated and shows no sign of slowing down.

Managers must therefore acquire the necessary skills to cope with change and must recognize that change presents *two* challenges for the modern manager. These are:

◆ Managing successfully while change is taking place. This often requires the manager to shoot at a moving target or at goal posts that have already been moved.

◆ Contributing to the successful introduction of change (i.e., keeping the ball in play while assisting with the planning and execution of the task of moving the goal posts).

The diagram on the following page illustrates the nature of change.

◆ *Present situation* is where we are now.

◆ *Desired future situation* is where we intend to be in the future, for example with new systems, new policies, new structures, new or additional premises, or new staffing arrangements. Between the two situations a *change* takes place.

◆ *Transitional period* is the time during which the changes take place; it is a critical period in managing change. *Strategies to achieve change* (which we will talk about in Chapter 3) are the ways in which we decide how to handle the forthcoming changes.

◆ *Resistances or obstacles* are essentially challenges to be overcome during the move from the present situation to the desired situation.

◆ *Time* runs from left to right. The following diagram is not intended to indicate how much time is available to give effect to the changes, but it is important during any particular period of change to take available time into account in formulating strategies.

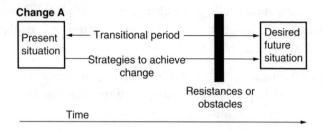

This diagram relates to one individual change. More than one change may be taking place at any one time and it is possible to be in several transitional periods at once, each in different stages. The manager has not only to keep the show on the road but may need to juggle several "change balls" at the same time. Each change that is taking place may require its own strategy.

The diagram on the following page may exaggerate the complexity of a situation embracing a number of changes, but it may not. The manager who copes with multiple changes successfully will be the one who has a clear perspective of the boundaries between the various changes that are taking place. We must not overlook the fact that two or more changes may be interrelated. They may be sub-changes of a complex pattern of change.

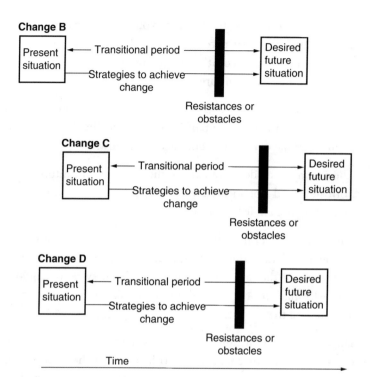

Change may also be likened to a transformation process that can be illustrated as follows:

◆ *Inputs* may be likened to the steps you take to change the furnishing and decor of a room (e.g., selection of a new color scheme, obtaining decorating materials, paper, paint, selecting and obtaining new furniture).

◆ The *transformation process* may include redecoration, replacing of carpets, and placement of new furniture in the room. We might even have moved or enlarged a window.

◆ The *outputs* include more light in the room and furniture that is both new and not located where its predecessors stood (e.g., Dad's favorite chair has been moved).

To illustrate this point using an example, the purchase of new equipment and investment in training would be the inputs; the introduction of the new equipment and related systems would be the transformation process; and a new invoicing system in operation would be the output.

Change is never-ending and, therefore, it is important to learn from successive periods of change. Try to learn from the changes that were carried out well in addition to those that were executed less effectively. We are usually prepared to learn from our mistakes but we seldom take the opportunity offered to learn from our successes. We must remember, however, that situations and circumstances may differ, and the lessons from one period of change may not be directly applicable in another. There is always a risk in seeking to solve a new problem with an old solution. The solution may not be appropriate—or worse still a misfit may not be recognized.

How did we get it right? Are there any lessons we can learn that will help us to get it right in the future? We can learn from failure but we must not concentrate on it to the exclusion of success.

Lessons identified from success are most likely to emerge when a successfully executed project follows one marked by problems.

What did we do differently? What contributed to our success this time?

Examples of lessons from failure

◆ Failure to plan ahead

◆ Failure to recognize how much and exactly what kind of training would be needed

◆ Failure to inform the staff—it was assumed that they would know without actually being told

◆ Failure to calculate the additional workload that would be generated during the transitional period

◆ Failure to recognize that the allocation of work during the transitional period would need to be defined carefully—too many jobs were left to chance

Examples of lessons from success

◆ Communication and consultation started early.

◆ Everyone concerned was involved—including those who were absent in the first phases.

◆ Other departments' interests were taken into account.

◆ A plan was drawn up that took account of the target date for completion of the change.

◆ The plan was amended as circumstances changed.

◆ Revisions to the plan were communicated to all involved.

◆

OBSTACLES TO MANAGING CHANGE EFFECTIVELY

Confronted with change, you need to be aware of potential obstacles. It may be impossible to do anything about them. If anything, that is a more compelling reason for being aware of them and of their likely impact. They include:

◆ Limitations of resources (e.g., staff, time, skills, equipment)

◆ An increasing workload, some routine and some (likely to be an increasing amount) generated by the change process, aggravating problems of limited time

◆ Lack of clear objectives and of bases for making local decisions, and difficulty in obtaining decisions from a higher level

◆ Resistance to change

◆ Lack of positive motivation on the part of staff

◆ Problems of communication—up, down, and across. We all like to blame "them" for not communicating. We forget that some-times *we* are "them." A good rule for each day is "*Who* do I need to tell *what?*"

◆ Large groups with differing levels of knowledge, experience, and competence that may:
  – aggravate the problems of communication and motivation
  – slow down the change process

◆ People's differing attitudes to change and to specific changes

COPING WELL WITH CHANGE

Research has shown that managers who cope well with change fre-quently have important qualities that distinguish them from less effective change managers. Managers who cope less well with change seem to be those who rely too heavily on prior experience and who are less flexible in their responses to the challenges of change.

Here we need to look at two groups of qualities—personal and managerial. It may be useful for managers, in situations embracing change, to measure themselves, their bosses, and their closest sub-ordinates discreetly against the features in the list that follows. They may not be able to change themselves, their bosses, or their staff, but they will have a general idea about the attitudinal prob-lems with which they may be confronted in bringing about change. Honesty is essential. Those of a conservative disposition should recognize this fact and not delude themselves that they are torch-bearing revolutionaries.

Personal qualities

Feature	More successful	Less successful
Orientation	Enthusiastic for growth, change, and new experience; takes risks; focused on ends	Prefers the status quo; lacks motivation; concerned for security; preoccupied with means
Sentiments	Open to more than one course of action	Believes in one best way
Work aspirations	Seeks and gives responsibility and interesting work; values achievement	Prefers regularity, order and financial security; seeks prestige and status
Leisure activities	Engaged in more diverse and less conventional activities	Enjoys limited and conventional interests

Managerial qualities

Feature	More successful	Less successful
Technical skills	Boss does not expect to be regarded as the technical expert	Boss considers self—and expects to be considered—as the technical expert
Leadership	Understands relationship between efficiency and human relations	Fails to understand relationship between efficiency and human relations
Superiors	Bases respect on their contribution and ability	Submissive
Subordinates	Treats as members of teams seeking to achieve common goals	Directive and authoritative
Decision	Relies on evidence rather than on experience	Uses old decisions for new probems

◆

FORCE FIELD ANALYSIS AND ITS RELEVANCE TO THE MANAGEMENT OF CHANGE

Force field analysis (FFA) is a technique for taking stock of the situation before embarking on change. It strives to identify:

◆ **driving forces** that tend to generate movement towards a goal

and

◆ **restraining forces or barriers** that inhibit movement towards a goal

An essential precondition of the analysis is determination of the desired goal.

What exactly are you trying to achieve?
What change are you trying to bring about?

Until you can answer those questions precisely you:

◆ can only achieve your goal by accident

◆ cannot carry out FFA—driving and restraining forces may vary from one goal to another

The aim of FFA is not to evaluate the validity of a goal or change, but to help determine the best way to achieve it.

FFA assumes that proposed change will take place in an environment including, for example:

◆ people

◆ values

◆ priorities

◆ relationships

◆ physical surroundings

◆ needs

◆ ambitions

◆ attitudes

◆ accepted norms

The environment may range from a shared office to a whole company. These are only examples. What is important for the purposes of FFA is to identify the boundaries of the environment in which the change will take place.

Forces should:

◆ Be expressed specifically

◆ Be related to persons or groups of persons and their points of influence

◆ Include potential forces as well as those that can be identified at the time of analysis

What are the benefits of the proposed change—and to whom are they beneficial? What are the disadvantages—and who will be the disadvantaged?

Identification of forces strongly for or against a proposed change can lead to consideration of questions such as:

Where and how can influence be exerted to support the driving forces or reduce the impact of those opposing change?

Would reducing a restraining force have a greater impact than reinforcing a driving force?

Let us assume that we are a board of directors. We propose to introduce a no smoking policy throughout the company. What are the likely driving forces? What are the likely restraining forces? What arguments can be deployed to weaken the restraining forces or reinforce the driving forces?

Some driving forces for the change

◆ nonsmokers

◆ health risks

- saving money

- cleaner air in offices

- general movement towards nonsmoking (e.g., buses, trains, theaters, and public places)

Some restraining forces

- addicts, especially of senior status

- effects on health (smokers unwilling to go through withdrawal)

- a social tool (offer to colleagues)

- smokers claim to need a 'fix' to be able to concentrate

- smokers fear that quitting will cause them to gain weight

SUMMARY

We have spent this chapter introducing ourselves to change, to some of its implications, and to some related topics.

We have looked at:

◆ The nature of change and a framework for understanding it

◆ Potential obstacles to managing change effectively

◆ Managers who cope more or less effectively than others with change

◆ Force Field Analysis as an aid to change

We can now begin to anticipate our approach to more change in our organization. Some of the questions we may consider are:

◆ What will be the major blocks?

◆ Who will be our strongest allies?

◆ Who will provide the most resistance?

◆ How can they be influenced?

◆ What opportunities will a period of change provide?

◆ What challenges will a period of change provide?

Chapter 2

Managing During Change

This chapter examines some of the problems of managing change in a transitional period. We will consider:

◆ People problems during a period of change:
  – uncertainty
  – uncontrolled expectations
  – levels of motivation
  – resistance to change
  – stress
  – role ambiguity
  – balancing hard and soft management
  – difficulties in responding to staff questions
  – impact of simultaneous changes
  – maintaining and perpetuating commitment to existing systems

◆ Some guidelines for managing change effectively

PEOPLE PROBLEMS DURING A PERIOD OF CHANGE

The transitional period extends from the time when change is announced to the time when change is successfully completed. It is a time when successful managers are those who can demonstrate ability in managing their peers and subordinates.

Uncertainty

Good change managers:

◆ Know that uncertainty may be worse than bad news

◆ Explain changes regularly and as fully as possible

◆ Communicate more often with their teams than in normal circumstances. An absence of communication is a more common problem than poor communication.

◆ Maintain consistency in communication, ensuring that:
   – their words and actions are consistent
   – their words and actions at one time are consistent with words and actions at other times

◆ Make or, where necessary, obtain decisions to minimize the extent and duration of uncertainty

The moral is to make every effort to ensure that any news of developments about proposed changes is communicated to the staff as quickly as possible.

When information affects only one individual, be sure to communicate it privately.

Uncontrolled expectations
Expectations must be controlled.

Good change managers know that:

◆ Expectations must be kept in perspective.

◆ Expectations should not be allowed to become too high or to remain too low.

◆ Unrealistic expectations may lead to a sense of anticlimax and lowered morale.

◆ Low expectations may lead to a lack of enthusiasm.

◆ Their own expectations must be kept under control and should be realistic.

◆ Their own moods and perceived moods can affect their teams.

◆ Excessive pessimism and complacency are equally bad.

One strategy to motivate staff is to paint a picture of better times ahead. This must not be overdone. If the promised benefits do not accrue it will be difficult to obtain a big effort on a future occasion.

Levels of motivation

The period of transition in a major change may last for 12 months or more. Even without the pending change, effort will be required from a manager to maintain motivation.

Good change managers know that:

◆ An enthusiastic approach does not just happen—it has to be cultivated and nurtured.

◆ The burden of sustaining enthusiasm will be increased during a period of frustration, difficulties, long hours, and perhaps, from time to time, weekend working.

◆ They have the additional burden of always projecting a positive attitude.

◆ They are only human and will share the frustrations and anxieties of those who are responsible to them.

◆ They must strive to conceal any negative emotions of their own in order to promote positive attitudes in others.

◆ They must demonstrate commitment, whatever they may feel inside, if they are to provide emotional support to their subordinates.

Managers sometimes seek to identify with their teams or gain their support by criticizing their own superiors and the decisions that they have taken. They overlook the fact that, if they do, it will only be a matter of time before team members criticize the managers themselves.

> *Whatever the manager's inner feelings it is important to promote positive attitudes.*

Good change managers recognize that their people are the greatest assets they have, especially during a period of change.

Good change managers therefore:

◆ Acknowledge achievement, but take action when deadlines are not met

◆ Are seen regularly and keep in touch with their teams, their feelings, problems and with progress, to a greater extent than usual

◆ Walk the job regularly and are available to staff on a regular basis

◆

Resistance to change

Resistance to change is a major problem that must be confronted positively. We will deal with this topic in greater detail in Chapters 4 and 5; all we will say for now is that resistance can seldom be overcome by edict. People cannot be instructed to welcome change.

Directives may lead to concealment of resistance but, by themselves, will not take away its causes. The manager must confront the underlying causes rather than the symptoms.

Stress

Again we mention stress at this point only for the sake of completeness. It is a topic to which we will return in Chapters 4 and 5. Stress—or fear of an inability to cope—is a major and often unrecognized cause of resistance to change.

Role ambiguity

As the changing situation unfolds, the tasks and responsibilities that make up individuals' roles or jobs will change.

Without proper control, chaos will develop. Without control, sooner or later, a task will fall between two people, each of whom thinks that it is the responsibility of the other. If necessary, daily meetings should be held to clarify issues about roles and responsibilities that have arisen under changing or new arrangements.

Examples of emerging changes

◆ Part of John's job may disappear.

◆ Mary may acquire tasks that she did not have before.

◆ Colleagues may gain responsibilities from both.

Good change managers pay particular attention to:

◆ Keeping the definition and communication of roles under constant review

◆ Individual needs for training and coaching as roles evolve

Balancing hard and soft management

People problems may arise when managers fail to strike an appropriate balance between hard and soft management.

Change requires:

◆ sympathetic, encouraging, and understanding attitudes on the part of managers

◆ firm decisions and responses

◆ clear direction

◆ a capacity and disposition to sometimes say 'no'

There is a danger that a perceived need for soft management may lead to giving directions, decisions, and responses (especially "no") in ambiguous terms in a misguided attempt to soften their impact. This is in no one's best interest, least of all that of those misled.

Difficulties in responding to staff questions

Staff will undoubtedly ask questions to which answers are not yet available. If an answer is not available you should admit it and not pretend that staff cannot be informed because "it is confidential to management." Managers must not adopt this strategy to conceal their own ignorance.

Good change managers know that:

◆ It may be necessary to seek answers to questions.

◆ If promises are made, then those promises must be kept.

◆ If time elapses, then those concerned should be reassured that responses are still being sought.

◆ When a response must be delayed the staff should be informed.

◆ Staff will lose confidence in a manager who appears to be delaying a response.

Impact of simultaneous changes

People problems may be aggravated by simultaneous changes taking place externally or outside the control of local management. In Chapter 1 we illustrated a situation in which several changes were occurring simultaneously. In a case like this the changes may or may not be related to each other, but in either case it is not difficult to imagine the complexity of the people problems that may arise.

Examples of external causes include:

◆ Changes in government policy that may have an impact on the business environment

◆ Legal changes that may impose new or increased burdens on business activity

People problems that may arise include:

◆ Staff resignations (which tend to increase during a period of heightened uncertainty)

◆ Difficulty in filling vacancies (a period of major change and uncertainty may not be attractive)

◆ Confusion as the elements of the various changes become blurred

Multiple changes may extend tolerance to a breaking point.

Maintaining and perpetuating commitment to existing systems

Difficulties may arise when existing and new systems and procedures operate in parallel. It may be necessary to divert staff from the existing system to prepare for changing to the new system.

Good change managers know that:

◆ This may impose a strain on staff who are required to work harder and longer.

◆ This will cause its own operational problems and may generate apathy from those with uncertain futures.

◆ Staff cannot be expected to devote their best efforts to creating a situation that may lead to redundancy, demotion, or to what they see as adverse change.

Another aspect of this situation will be the need to maintain commitment to systems and procedures that the staff may already recognize as obsolete.

They may progressively:

◆ Seek shortcuts

◆ Become casual in keeping records

◆ Be careless in maintaining equipment

◆ Defer work in the hope that the new system will make it easier or even redundant

- ◆ Become indifferent to procedures

- ◆ Allow filing to accumulate

- ◆ Assume less diligent attitudes, particularly towards routine tasks

It may be difficult to maintain standards at such a time. Any down-hill trend must be arrested quickly.

Good change managers know that it is important to:

- ◆ Regularly emphasize the need to maintain standards

- ◆ Discourage staff from lapsing into a sense of false security and adopting lax ways

- ◆ Walk the job more frequently

- ◆ Make snap inspections of records and output to demonstrate a commitment to the present systems

Good change managers therefore:

- ◆ Subordinate personal feelings in demonstrating commitment to existing systems and to change

- ◆ Encourage team commitment by setting interim targets of achievement for both existing systems and the change process

- ◆ Maintain control using regular checks to measure progress against the plan for change

There is no specific way of dealing with these problems. It is impor-tant that you are aware of them, look for them, and take action when they arise. Do not take members of your team for granted, nor make assumptions about their attitudes, nor communicate doubt to them. You know how much you like to complain among yourselves about "they"—"they don't tell us anything; they don't seem to know that we are . . ." Remember that, to your teams, you are part of "they."

Good change managers know that:

◆ Involvement of the staff should not be seen as an option—it should be recognized as essential.

◆ Change takes time and resources.

◆ Time and resources must be used to the best advantage.

◆ Planning and foresight may not eliminate people problems, but can do much to minimize them.

SOME GUIDELINES FOR MANAGING CHANGE EFFECTIVELY

There are no hard and fast rules for managing change, but some principles worth considering have emerged from successful change operations. Few of us approach change with confidence.

Our guidelines do not represent a panacea. They are not offered prescriptively. There may, for example, be situations in which it is not possible to involve the staff as much as you wish. That does not mean, however, that you should not consider how much you can involve them and that you should not involve them to the maximum, however little that may be.

Few managers can be certain of the direction they should take throughout a period of change. However, good change managers should:

◆ Work hard to establish and demonstrate the need for and the advantages of changes (whatever their personal feelings may be)

◆ Think through proposed changes:
 – Will they alter job content?
 – Will they introduce new and unknown tasks?
 – Will they disrupt established methods of working?
 – Will they affect group relationships both within and between groups?
 – Will they reduce or extend limits of authority?
 – Will they lower status for some individuals?
 – How much explanation or discussion is needed?
 – Who will be most affected?
 – What training may be needed?

◆ Initiate change, as much as possible, in ways that involve the staff as a team and that do not leave them feeling used as a means of getting things done, rather than as contributors to the total change process

◆ Encourage a full airing of objections and deal with them on their merits

◆ Avoid pretending to seek revisions to the changes proposed unless they intend to do so

◆ Know that words and actions must be consistent

◆ Be prepared to make changes themselves and to listen to ideas from their subordinates

◆ Recognize that a number of heads are better than one

◆ Value the contributions that others, perhaps "closer to the action," can make

◆ Remember that no one has a monopoly on knowledge or wisdom

◆ Monitor progress through changes and reinforce that progress, recognizing that change will not happen but must be made to happen

These guidelines are not exhaustive. Good change managers think through changes as far in advance as possible. Success will reward their efforts if they do so.

SUMMARY

We have considered people problems including:

◆ Uncertainty and uncontrolled expectations

◆ Levels of motivation and resistance

◆ Role ambiguity

◆ Balancing hard and soft management

◆ Difficulties in responding to staff questions

◆ Simultaneous changes

◆ Commitment to existing systems

We have also looked at some guidelines for managers. An old dictum declares that "if we look after the people, the changes will look after themselves." This statement may not be entirely true, but it goes a long way towards identifying the real problem in managing change—managing people.

It may be useful to use the organizations in which you find yourselves as laboratories. Some of your colleagues will be successful and respected in managing their teams, others less so.

◆ What differentiates them?

◆ What lessons can you learn?

◆ What makes Susan a good manager?
  – What qualities and attributes does she display?

◆ What makes Bill less successful as a supervisor?
  – What qualities and attributes does he display?

Chapter 3

Strategies for Managing Change

This chapter examines strategies for managing change. Major change seldom arrives without notice and successful managers will consider the following factors in advance:

◆ Selecting an overall management style

◆ Increasing readiness for change

◆ Communicating about change

◆ Adjusting the balance of those for and against change

◆ Choosing strategies appropriate to the time available

The period of advance warning is precious. It enables you to prepare and above all to formulate strategies for dealing with the forthcoming change.

What do we mean by *strategies* for managing change? Let us assume we have been told that the organization is to introduce major changes (e.g., changes to the computer system or to the locations of certain departments or functions). Our superior may have decided to introduce changes. We may have decided to change things at our own level.

Choosing strategies for managing change means, essentially, deciding how to handle it. A strategy contains a number of interrelated elements such as those listed at the beginning of this chapter.

The amount of choice to be made at local level varies. In the event of a change to be introduced organization-wide, the room for maneuver at local level may be limited. However, each of these elements should be considered at local level, each time change is introduced.

Senior management may have decided to communicate by memo. There are still options to be considered and choices to be made about how staff are to be informed. They might each be given a copy of the memo; a copy of the memo might be put on the bulletin board; an abbreviated memo might be prepared at local level including only information relevant to the staff in that branch or department; meetings might be held of section heads or of all staff using the memo as a script.

However limited the discretion of local management, the elements of a strategy should always be considered because:

◆ There is usually some discretion.

◆ There is often more discretion than may appear to be the case at first sight.

◆ It is important that the discretion is recognized and exercised wisely if the change is to be introduced in the most effective way.

SELECTING AN OVERALL MANAGEMENT STYLE

Available styles can be ranked in order of the amount of influence retained by management or given to the staff. Possible styles include:

Management tells

The change is announced and the staff are informed that they will carry out the necessary actions. This style is based on the premise that "it is management's job to manage."

Advantages
Quick; unambiguous; decisive

Disadvantages
Danger of resentment; does not use staff's ideas or experience

Management tells and sells

The change is announced but efforts are made to persuade staff of its benefits and to reassure them.

Advantage
Management still feels in control

Disadvantage
May be seen as a cosmetic exercise if the change has serious negative effects on the staff

Management consults

Proposals for change are announced and comments and views of the staff are sought. Management makes the final decision.

Advantages
More information should lead to better decisions; greater staff commitment, especially if it is obvious that their views have influenced decisions

Disadvantages
Time-consuming; resentment of staff if views seem to be ignored

Management invites participation

Staff are invited to join in reaching decisions about change and its introduction. Participation thus goes further than consultation and differs from negotiation. Management and staff act as joint problem solvers.

Advantages
Uses all information available leading to best decision; greater degree of commitment from staff who share ownership of decisions

Disadvantages
Time-consuming; problems of mechanics; conflicts with ideas of managerial accountability; management has least control over outcome

Negotiation
Negotiation is included for completeness only. The extent to which negotiation takes place and at what level depends on arrangements existing between organizations and trade unions.

Choosing a style
In selecting a change management style, remember:

◆ There is no best style. The preferred style depends on the situation.

◆ Where there is a lengthy and complex change a combination of styles may be appropriate (e.g., tell and sell the change); invite participation in reaching decisions about implementation.

INCREASING READINESS FOR CHANGE
There are three basic tactics to increase staff readiness for change. These are:

1. Focus on disadvantages of the present situation

   or

2. Build a vision of a better state of affairs

   or

3. Combine approaches 1 and 2.

Examples of disadvantages of the current situation are:

◆ excessive overtime

◆ confused lines of communication

◆ remote management

◆ obsolete equipment

◆ uncertainty about the future

◆ unfairness of pay structure

You can highlight a better state of affairs that might include:

◆ better working conditions

◆ more opportunities for promotion

◆ greater job security as the organization becomes more competitive

◆ a greater degree of equity in evaluating and rewarding staff

◆ easier access to shopping facilities

You know that a given change is coming. You can consider, in advance, how you can increase readiness for change. You can then be consistent in what you say to your staff, rather than making it up as you go along.

Training

In a situation of major change, plans for training may be made centrally. What additional training may be needed locally? Who will do it? How will they be equipped to provide this training? What provision may be necessary for *ad hoc* training if there are staff changes during the change period? How can supervisors be trained before those they supervise to give them an edge of expertise? What new knowledge will be needed? What new or enhanced skills will be required? Do attitudes need to be influenced (e.g., will there be a premium on teamwork or more opportunities for individual initiative)?

Suitable timely training can contribute greatly to increased readiness for change.

COMMUNICATING ABOUT CHANGE

There are four key questions to answer before you communicate about change:

◆ **Who** needs to be told?

◆ **What** should they be told?

◆ **When** should they be told?

◆ **How** should they be told?

Who?

Everyone who will be affected directly or indirectly by the change. Be aware of the danger of excluding anyone in a small unit or group. Exclusion may lead to resentment.

◆ Do people outside the unit need to be told (e.g., customers or other departments)?

What?

You should communicate as much information as possible in order to:

◆ Respect the intelligence of subordinates and to win their trust and respect

◆ Get ahead of the grapevine that may provide more complete information

◆ Ensure that inaccurate rumors do not fill information gaps

You should cover:

◆ What will be changed

◆ Why it is being changed

◆ What the implications are

◆ The likely timescale

◆ The ways in which staff may be involved

◆ Guarantees or reassurances—where possible

When?
You should communicate:

◆ As soon as possible after decisions have been made (subject to confidentiality)

◆ Continuously, as required, after the first announcement (communication of, and about, change is not a one-time event but an ongoing process)

How?

Orally? Should we communicate orally one-to-one, to subgroups, or to the whole group?

Advantages
Modification possible in light of reactions; questions can be answered

Disadvantages
No communication with absentees; difficult to ensure that subgroups all receive same message unless same messenger is used

In writing? Should we communicate by letter, by memo, or by using the bulletin board?

Advantages
Total coverage; standard message

Disadvantages
Different interpretations possible unless memo drafted unambiguously; no immediate reactions

However, it should be noted that oral and written communication are *not* mutually exclusive. A memo can be followed up later by a meeting; a memo may be used to reinforce what is said at a meeting.

Visually? Don't forget that drawings and diagrams can supplement written and oral communication (e.g., to demonstrate new office layouts).

ADJUSTING THE BALANCE OF
THOSE FOR AND AGAINST CHANGE

You must always think through the change. Who will be most affected? Who is likely to be most resistant, least cooperative, or just apathetic? Seek to win over the apathetic first; they should be more easily persuaded. Their conversion increases the number of those favoring change.

You must involve the staff if you are to succeed in adjusting the balance. There are other reasons for devoting time to this. They include:

◆ Demonstrating respect for them and gaining their trust and respect in return

◆ Gaining their commitment

◆ Obtaining the benefits of their detailed knowledge

◆ Gaining access to an early warning system. The staff may see indirect adverse consequences of the change before they happen and before management does.

The types of involvement include:

◆ Directive communication—may cause apathy

◆ Consultation (seeking staff views)—deadlines may not permit and the consultation may appear cosmetic

◆ Consulting staff representatives—how to select; may not be truly representative; may alienate others

◆ Staff participation in development of plan for change—time-consuming but makes best use of all available knowledge

CHOOSING STRATEGIES APPROPRIATE TO THE TIME AVAILABLE

Time is a continuum. When should change take place?

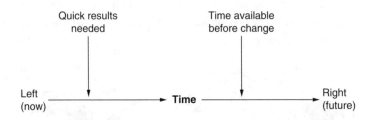

In the above diagram, a movement to the left means bringing change forward in time and a movement to the right implies a delay to the change.

Consider the following points when deciding on the timing of change:

Time available

◆ Quick results needed—LEFT

◆ Change not imminent or urgent—RIGHT

◆ Significant obstacles—RIGHT

Management/staff relationships

◆ Mutual trust exists—LEFT

◆ Trust must be won—RIGHT

At stake

◆ Crisis—LEFT

◆ Time not at a premium; effective change more important than time—RIGHT

Compromise may be necessary. Even in the absence of mutual trust a crisis requires immediate action.

SUMMARY

In the course of this chapter we have learned:

◆ The importance of determining strategies for managing change in advance

◆ The choices available in selecting an overall management style during the period of change

◆ An approach to increasing the readiness for change on the part of those involved

◆ The choices available in communicating about the forthcoming changes

◆ The importance of adjusting the balance of those for and against change, and the role of staff involvement in this process

◆ The relationship between time available and the choice of strategy

Above all, change requires careful, detailed planning—you cannot rely on making it up as you go along.

Chapter 4

Resistance to
Change

In this chapter we will examine another aspect of change—resistance to change and its causes. We will focus on the causes of resistance and consider how to deal with that resistance.

Our topics will include:

◆ Forms of resistance to change
  – the importance of understanding causes of resistance

◆ Fear and factors that generate it
  – perceived threats to intrinsic benefits
  – perceived threats to extrinsic rewards
  – perceived conflicts with other roles
  – resistance based on misunderstanding
  – perceived threats to group cohesion
  – perceived threats generated by the way change is introduced
  – those most likely to resist change

FORMS OF RESISTANCE TO CHANGE

Change takes many forms and reactions to change similarly take many forms. However, it is rare for change not to be accompanied by at least a degree of resistance, even if it is only passive.

Minor and major change

Let's consider change at two ends of the scale. First, take the case of Norman, the company's representative in Hawaii, who has authority to determine the prices for customers there. Mike in the sales office is kept aware of Norman's pricing structure and is so familiar with it that he has never written it down. Norman is retiring and the sales manager has decided that it is not acceptable that Mike alone knows the price structure. He insists that the Hawaiian prices are written down and circulated to all the sales office staff. Mike resents the change that will reduce his power. He knows his indispensability will disappear and resists the change by constantly lying about writing the price structure down.

At the other end of the scale there is a situation where company X has successfully bid for company Y, the operations of which will be merged into those of company X. Panic, apprehension and misunderstanding prevail in company Y, and people become apathetic about the day-to-day activities that they expect will become the subject of change. Their apathy is an expression of their resistance to those changes.

Resistance may take as many forms as change itself. Change may be confronted by:

Outright opposition to the proposed change and a refusal to adopt prescribed changes.

This is likely to occur infrequently, and in extreme cases disciplinary action may be the only remedy. Resistance by an individual is seldom pursued this far. The "Mikes" of this world recognize that, while they may get away with one more trip to Hawaii to sort out a complex customer account, they will have to toe the line eventually. Mass resistance is extremely unlikely to take place unless a trade union or representative body is involved and this is an aspect of resistance to change that lies outside the scope of this book.

However, resistance is likely to take more subtle forms, such as:

◆ uncooperative attitudes

◆ apathy

◆ reluctance to do things in new ways

◆ a reduced pace of work

◆ outspoken criticism voiced to colleagues rather than to superiors

◆ formulation and spreading of unfounded rumors

◆ procrastination in giving effect to change

◆ attempts to persuade management to extend a period of consultation

Suggestions will be made for setting up committees, subcommittees, working parties, and other similar devices to consider or reconsider the merits of the changes themselves and their implementation. Debating how changes will be introduced is frequently the last resort of those seeking to resist change. This is not to deny the valuable role that those closest to the action can play in smoothing the path of change. We are referring to debate with the object of delay or obstruction rather than discussion aimed at facilitating the introduction of better ways and new structures.

The importance of understanding causes of resistance

Managers should understand likely causes of resistance for two reasons:

Before and after

◆ Managers who can understand and recognize the potential roots of resistance are better able to anticipate it and to take preventive action to eliminate or minimize it before it becomes a serious problem.

◆ Likewise managers who are aware of likely causes can tackle those causes rather than the symptoms after resistance has become apparent.

An understanding of the roots of resistance can thus be useful before resistance develops and in situations where it has already become a problem.

FEAR AND FACTORS THAT GENERATE IT

Much resistance to change is based on fear. Fear comes from uncertainty. It may or may not be well founded but, to those experiencing fear, it is very real. Some managers bury their heads in the sand like ostriches and pretend that fear does not exist among their staff because they believe that there is no cause for them to be afraid. They are unlikely to manage change successfully. Much fear of change is based upon misconceptions about the implications of changes, which is why two-way communication is especially essential in a period of change. Good managers do, of course, recognize that good communication—keeping the staff fully informed and knowing what is happening and how the staff feel about things—is important for effective operation at all times, not only in periods of change. In the latter it is vital.

A major change is announced. It may, for example, be a takeover or merger. It may be the disbandment of a large department, the functions of which may be redistributed throughout the parent organization. Such an announcement is seldom detailed—a bland statement, qualified only by an indication that further information will be issued later, is circulated. Among the questions that will concern those potentially involved are questions about the intrinsic benefits of their jobs. These questions will occur to people in random order. People who are afraid seldom think systematically.

Perceived threats to intrinsic benefits
Will proposed changes result in:

◆ Reduced job satisfaction?

◆ Reduced authority?

◆ Reduced variety of tasks?

◆ Reduced opportunities to socialize with present colleagues?

◆ Reduced status—actual or perceived?

◆ A need to make new relationships?

◆ Loss of existing skills that become redundant?

◆ A need to develop new and more complex skills?

◆ "The way we have always done things" being changed?

◆ Disruption of established comfortable superior/subordinate relationships ("Will I have a new boss?")?

Frightened people may ask some or all of these questions. They may ask them in any order. They may not ask them at all. People may conceal their fears. Questions about intrinsic benefits may be mixed up in people's minds with questions about the extrinsic rewards attached to their jobs. What are extrinsic rewards?

Perceived threats to extrinsic rewards
What impact will the changes have on:

◆ Pay in all its aspects—basic pay, overtime rates, and opportunities for overtime?

◆ Pension arrangements?

◆ Holiday entitlements?

◆ Provision of company cars?

◆ The security of the job itself?

Fundamental to the threat to extrinsic rewards are the questions:

Will I be able to pay the rent?
or
Will I be able to keep up my mortgage payments?

Good change managers recognize that the sooner questions about intrinsic benefits and extrinsic rewards can be answered the better.

They also recognize that the threat of change may generate fear about conflicts between workers' present and future roles and conflict with other roles in their lives.

Perceived conflicts with other roles
Other roles may include, for example, parent, club member, son with disabled parents, as opposed to roles within the organization.

Will changes mean:

◆ Longer hours? This may mean less time to spend with the family or for leisure activities.

◆ Less convenient hours? This may make it more difficult to pursue social activities.

◆ More difficult travel arrangements? These may result in more expense or, of themselves, have an impact on the time available for outside interests.

◆ Relocation of home? Fear of the need to relocate home and of its consequences on friendships, schooling, club membership, and so on, can justifiably dominate the thoughts of those likely to be affected.

All these considerations can have an adverse impact on performance, some permanent and some lasting, at least until, and if, the realities of the new situation are seen to be more agreeable than expected. That dreaded move to a different part of the country may be the start of a period of new opportunity.

Resistance based on misunderstanding

An individual may misunderstand the nature of the proposed change and its implications. Rumor may have persuaded Fred mistakenly that he will be required to move to another part of the country or become redundant. A good change manager will seek to clarify the cause of Fred's concern. This may not prevent Fred from worrying, but it may ensure that he worries about the right things, which may not be as serious as the things over which he is concerned.

Perceived threats to group cohesion

Most organizations subdivide into groups. Some groups are formal, for example, departments made up of people doing similar or related work. Some are informal, including, for example, people who belong to the organization's softball team. Change, or the possibility of it, may be seen as a threat to group cohesion. It will therefore be unwelcome and resisted. Some of the questions that may arise are:

Groups and change

◆ Will the change break up the group?

◆ Will an informal leader's opposition to change, based on personal reasons, influence the rest of the group?

◆ Will a group's shared interests be threatened?

◆ Will differentials between groups be changed?

◆ Will the identification of an individual with functional/task groups be threatened?

◆ Will identification with informal groups (people we may have lunch/coffee with) be threatened?

There is another potential cause of resistance—reaction to the way in which change is introduced as opposed to the change itself.

Perceived threats generated by the way change is introduced
The way change is introduced may have more impact than the change itself. We have all heard comments like, "I don't really mind what they've done, but it's the way they went about it—they could have asked us."

Examples of clumsy introduction of change include:

◆ insufficient notice of intended change

◆ insufficient consultation about intended change

◆ insufficient information about management's intentions and about the reasons for the change

We are considering again examples of delayed or insufficient communication or, worse still, a complete absence of communication. Whether inadequate communication is the result of carelessness or of design, it will generate a lack of confidence in management's ability or cynicism about its intentions, or both. Neither will facilitate the change process.

You now have insight into the reasons why groups and individuals oppose change. Absence of indication of any personal benefit ("What's in it for me?" "Why should I...?") and lack of trust or confidence in management ("Have they told us the whole story?") will aggravate opposition and resistance to change, generate resentment, and erode morale.

Fears may be unfounded but until staff are fully informed they tend to make assumptions—usually interpreting the situation in the least favorable way.

Given this background, is it surprising that many people oppose change, preferring the existing situation to a vague future in which there may not be a place for them or in which their role may be diminished and their interests may be prejudiced?

> *Dealing with resistance to change is perhaps the greatest challenge of managing change.*

Those most likely to resist change

You must avoid creating stereotypes; individuals may react unexpectedly to changing circumstances. Nevertheless, a good change manager knows that people in certain categories are more likely than others to resist change.

Resistance is most likely to come from:

◆ Those who are older and in the latter stages of their careers, who fear they may not be able to adapt and probably don't want to try

◆ The less well-educated, who may not understand the need for change and may fear their own redundancies

◆ The less competent, who may share the same fear

◆ Those at a lower level in the organization (i.e., more junior staff), who will usually be the least well informed and may be influenced by the fears expressed by older and more senior colleagues

SUMMARY

We have learned about and noted:

◆ The reasons why people resist change

◆ The forms that resistance may take

◆ The characteristics of those who appear to be most resistant to change

To be good change managers you must:

◆ Be aware of those factors in your environments that may cause resistance to change.

◆ Recognize behavior that may reflect such resistance.

◆ Identify cause and effect relationships so that you may attack the causes rather than the symptoms of resistance.

◆ Lend sympathetic support to those who are most vulnerable as change unfolds.

Above all you must recognize that resistance to change is part of the normal human condition. Which of us has not experienced a moment of rebellion on finding someone else in our usual place?

Chapter 5

Dealing with Resistance to Change

In this chapter we begin by considering stress, or more precisely, too much stress. We will look at what causes this condition and an individual's likely reaction to it. One possible reaction is resistance to an impending change.

We will also explain ways of dealing with resistance based on causes other than stress. Often your objective can only be to reduce rather than eliminate resistance to change. Nevertheless, it is always desirable to reduce the "temperature." Most things, including change, are better achieved in a situation that is not dominated by emotion.

We will explore these issues:

◆ Stress and its likely effects

◆ Managers' responses to stress

◆ Dealing with resistance to change
  – knowing your people
  – the role of communication
  – the role of education
  – involvement and participation
  – support by managers
  – selling the advantages of change
  – directing or ordering change

STRESS AND ITS LIKELY EFFECTS

Stress and change often go hand in hand. We are all subject to stress in varying degrees and need it to enable us to function.

What is stress? Stress is the condition in which individuals feel that they are under pressure and unable to cope. They have a low tolerance towards specific pressures and, perhaps, to pressure in general. The feeling that their grip on things is weakening constantly increases. Each new problem or unwelcome incident, however trivial, only confirms the feeling that things are out of control and, worse, that they may never be brought under control again.

Managers must recognize stress in their subordinates and help them to recognize it and take appropriate action. A good indicator of stress is an extended departure from a person's normal pattern of behavior.

Stress usually results from:

◆ Uncertainty about what is happening

◆ A perception, which may or may not be exaggerated, of the importance of what is happening (the exaggeration does not matter—what matters is the perception itself)

◆ Perceptions of a lack of ability to control and influence matters

In Chapter 4 we identified those most likely to resist change. Their resistance may not result from stress. We have already seen that a range of factors contribute to group or individual resistance. Good change managers will, however, carefully watch those in the categories that we identified for signs of stress. Such managers will not, of course, ignore their other charges. We are talking of priorities, but the order of priority is not fixed. There may be those who do not fit our stereotypes but who also find change hard to accept and therefore stressful for a variety of reasons.

Thus we have:

High level of uncertainty
+ *Perceived high level of*   *all*
  importance of changes, activities,   *contribute to*
  involvement, incidental   *STRESS*
  and even trivial happenings
+ *Perceived low and diminishing*
  level of ability to influence and
  control events and to cope

Stress is often summed up by those who feel it in such terms as, "I just can't cope" or "I don't know if or how I'll be able to cope."

Stress affects individuals rather than groups, but it is infectious. It is unlikely that the strains and pressures of change will affect all members of a group in the same way. Individual personal circumstances vary widely as do relative levels of emotional resilience.

Likely reactions to stress, by those affected, include:

◆ physical and mental illness

◆ apathy

◆ low self-esteem

◆ exhaustion

◆ loss of confidence

◆ anxiety

◆ insomnia

◆ aggression

◆ defensive attitudes

◆ uncertainty compensated for by
  - generating or retelling rumors, "We don't know the facts—let's make them up."
  - seeking information—repeated or anxious inquiry may be indicative of stress

◆ behavioral characteristics such as:
  - bad timekeeping
  - reduced standards of performance
  - increased smoking or consumption of alcohol
  - unwillingness to delegate
  - irrational problem solving
  - withdrawal—a developing pattern of absence, seeking a transfer, or even resigning

In any given situation stress may be the cause of resistance. You should, however, also consider other possible causes.

Some of those who suffer from stress may of course display a more positive approach and make efforts to learn how to control their place in the scheme of things. They don't deserve to be ignored because they are trying to cope with their problems rather than conceding defeat.

MANAGERS' RESPONSES TO STRESS

A good change manager will:

◆ Create opportunities for people, individually and collectively, to express their fears and worries, and will listen sympathetically.

◆ Keep close enough to the staff to be aware of unfounded rumors that may be circulating and counter those rumors whenever possible.

◆ Provide regular information about changes and their progress— but will remember that this alone will not remove uncertainty (only direct experience can do that).

◆ Involve the staff in planning the introduction of the changes as much as possible.

◆ Ensure that no one feels left out.

◆ Look for signs of stress in individuals.

◆ Counsel those having difficulties, helping them manage their own stress.

◆ Report to senior management or the personnel department when an individual's condition seems chronic.

During a period of major change a manager has many additional burdens. Our suggestions about what a good change manager should do adds to those burdens. However, staff morale and welfare demand the highest priority. Time spent with staff is an investment. It may seem easy to postpone those tasks that relate to staff and to appear to take the staff for granted. It is so easy to say, Linda is looking worried. I'll have a word with her tomorrow. Tomorrow may never come. It is so easy to think that it might be a good idea to assemble everyone to review progress—next week. Next week is further away than tomorrow and may never come either.

Stress is real to those suffering from it. However, managers must not assume that every frown or worried expression indicates a condition requiring professional attention. If you are in doubt about an individual case you must refer the matter upwards or to those in charge of personnel matters so that a clinical condition does not become aggravated by your indifference.

It is also important to pass information about staff attitudes and morale regularly to the relevant people.

DEALING WITH RESISTANCE TO CHANGE

Knowing your people

Countering resistance to change requires a range of skills and attitudes. In part they add up to the ability to manage people well. Basic to this requirement is that managers should know their people and that their people should know them.

◆ We are not advocating excessive familiarity or contact, or intrusive behavior by managers.

◆ We are not prescribing interference in the relationships between your subordinates and the staff who report to them.

◆ Do not create confusion in the chain of command by issuing instructions or receiving messages over the heads of your immediate subordinates.

◆ Do not encroach on their responsibilities or privileges nor undermine their authority.

You must, however, know your people as human beings. To do this, find the time to talk to them individually and informally from time to time. Remember that you can delegate management and supervision, but you cannot delegate leadership. You cannot lead people who don't know you and trust you.

The time to get to know your people is now—before major change occurs.

The role of communication

Constant efforts should be made to improve communication at all times whether or not change is taking place.

Good change managers:

◆ Regularly develop channels of communication

◆ Communicate effectively to reduce levels of uncertainty and hinder rumors when change is expected

They consider:

◆ Who needs to be told

◆ What they should be told

◆ When they should be told

◆ How they should be told

As much as possible they tell the staff:

◆ What is going to change

◆ Why the change is considered necessary

◆ What its implications are

◆ What the likely timescale is

They will, as much as possible, give reassurances on:

◆ redundancy

◆ earnings

◆ transfer

◆ relocation

They will recognize:

◆ The need to show respect for the staff and for their intelligence

◆ The importance of all groups learning about changes simultaneously

◆ The importance of the staff receiving news from management and not, for example, from the local press, radio, or television

◆ Communication about change is a continuous process

The role of education

We advocate educating staff in several ways before change occurs, which will make resistance less likely or more easily dealt with if it emerges.

Your first aim should be to promote understanding of the pressures in the working environment that may lead to significant change.

Your second aim should be to create awareness of what is actually happening or is likely to happen. Lastly help your people put change into a reasonable and accurate perspective. The introduction of an electric pencil sharpener, for example, should not lead to stress and resistance if people are well managed.

External pressures include:

◆ legal and political

◆ economic

◆ social and cultural

◆ technological

◆ competitors' activities

◆ customers' demands

Internal pressures usually stem from:

◆ strategic decisions (perhaps taken in response to external pressures)

◆ internal political conflict

◆ organizational structures that hinder rather than help

◆ lack of flexibility

◆ inadequacy of equipment

These pressures will produce responses in the form of changes. People who understand the pressures and can directly relate changes to them are more likely to understand, be aware of, and accommodate change than to resist it.

By education we mean a gradual process of helping people to understand the pressures to which the organization may be subjected and the interrelationships between pressures and changes. The likelihood of change coming as a complete shock is reduced and capacities to respond positively will be strengthened. The need for the firm to survive, adapt, and grow will be recognized.

Trust and mutual confidence will be enhanced.

Involvement and participation of staff
Good change managers know that:

◆ They may need to change their own behavior to support the staff in the change process.

◆ Change will be more effective and the staff more satisfied, or less disturbed, if they are fully involved in a way that releases all their capacities to supplement the efforts of management.

◆ Old-fashioned direction and obedience will not result in change being achieved in the most effective way.

◆ The attitude of staff will change only if the attitude of management is seen to change.

◆ Involving the staff does not mean abdication by management.

◆ Effective change means seeking (not demanding) the opinions of those closest to the action about how management decisions (partly based on views provided by the staff) should be implemented.

◆ Staff who feel they have a degree of ownership of decisions will implement them with greater commitment.

Gaining the involvement and support of staff requires:

◆ above all, listening

◆ training to give staff knowledge, skill, and confidence

◆ counseling

◆ an investment in time

Support by managers
This may take the form of:

◆ providing training to give staff knowledge, skills, and confidence

◆ counseling staff

◆ listening

Providing support requires an investment in time. Every effort should be made to provide this support. In a period of change a confident and well-motivated staff is a manager's greatest asset.

Selling the advantages of change

Make every effort to sell staff the advantages of change. But be careful—if there is opposition to change it may not be helpful to sell them the advantages unless these can be expressed in terms of advantages to the staff. People who are going to be subjected to inconvenience and stress with no immediate advantages are unlikely to be impressed with arguments suggesting that "the changes will enable management to exercise a greater degree of control" or that the organization will be more efficient.

When selling the benefits of change, talk to your people in terms of their advantage—where there is a real advantage—and not in terms of advantages to management or the firm.

When appropriate, it may be useful to explain how change can benefit jobs. Change may provide:

◆ greater opportunities for self-fulfillment

◆ improved responsibilities and prospects

◆ a favorable change of environment

◆ new challenges

◆ improved career prospects

◆ opportunities to acquire new skills and knowledge—to become more marketable and more capable of being promoted

Directing or ordering change

There may be circumstances in which it is necessary to tell, instruct, or order those staff who may be opposed to change to adopt different procedures or practices. This approach takes the minimum amount of time and should be seriously considered where little time is available.

This need not be done harshly, but it must be done firmly and unambiguously. It will solve the immediate problem, but it is unlikely to remove deep-rooted resistance or opposition to change. Counseling and listening may still be necessary (or even more necessary than normal) when time becomes available.

Be careful not to introduce the prospect of reversing the change, or even of considering reversal. If this is suggested and does not follow, trust and mutual confidence will be eroded. Worst of all, the respect of those who loyally adopted the change will be lost.

SUMMARY

In this chapter we have learned:

◆ How to understand the causes of stress and recognize its symptoms

◆ How managers can anticipate and respond to stress

◆ How managers can respond to resistance to change

◆ How these responses will be more effective if action is taken in advance to
  – know and be known by staff
  – develop effective lines of communication
  – educate staff, above all to help them see change in perspective

◆ How not to sell change and its advantages

◆ How to involve and support staff during change

◆ How to direct staff or order change when circumstances leave no choice

Chapter 6

The Psychological Impact of Change

In this section we will examine aspects of change often ignored when change is being planned or taking place. They are the psychological impact of change and the implications of change for the way in which staff are managed.

In particular we will consider:

◆ Four stages of the transitional period

◆ Likely behavior and appropriate responses

Change is a journey, not a destination. Good change managers recognize change as a journey and plan for change on that basis. This

in turn contributes to effective operation as change progresses. They also recognize that response to change is influenced by the way managers behave during—and perhaps more critically before—change.

FOUR STAGES OF THE TRANSITIONAL PERIOD

Managing change becomes easier if it is recognized that there are four distinct stages within the period of transition. There is general agreement among psychologists about the number of stages, less agreement about how to label them.

For example, one grouping is:

◆ shock

◆ resistance

◆ exploration

◆ commitment

Another is:

◆ shock and resistance

◆ confusion

◆ integration

◆ acceptance

We will use the latter as our basis for discussion. We will consider the likely behavior of those affected at each stage and the most appropriate responses from managers. This analysis will bring together many points that have been made under other headings and help to consolidate our understanding of the change process.

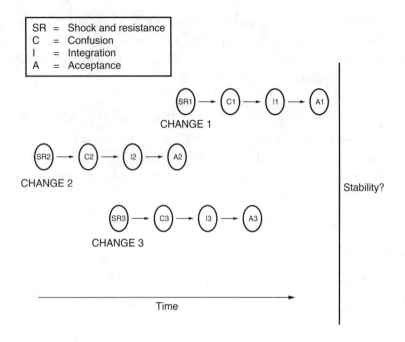

SR = Shock and resistance
C = Confusion
I = Integration
A = Acceptance

The diagram illustrates a situation in which one sequence

shock and resistance → acceptance

has been completed immediately before another cycle begins. Life, sadly, is not like that. A number of changes may be taking place at any time. One, for example, may have reached the confusion stage, while another is just about to reach acceptance, and so on. The diagram suggests that the lapse of time between one stage and another in each sequence is the same. Life is not like that either. Coping with multiple change is not easy, but it becomes easier if we recognize what is happening and can respond appropriately.

LIKELY BEHAVIOR AND APPROPRIATE RESPONSES

Shock and resistance—expected behaviors

◆ Change generates resistance.

◆ The status quo seems preferable to change, though the status quo may, itself, not be ideal.

◆ Fear of the unknown prevails.

◆ People are reluctant to lose familiar rituals, practices, and colleagues.

◆ Feelings of inadequacy may emerge as old roles are replaced by new roles with new demands.

◆ New patterns of interaction and loss of established relationships may add to feelings of resentment.

◆ Status and authority may seem to be under threat.

◆ There is a perception of rewards being under threat and of reduced opportunities for advancement.

◆ People may feel that change is being imposed and resent and resist the change to an even greater degree.

◆ People may opt out of trying to understand the change or to put it into perspective.

◆ Evidence of resentment and resistance may show itself in:
  – a high degree of stress
  – lack of awareness
  – anger
  – sadness
  – anxiety

- excessive caution
- stubborness
- withdrawal
- indifference
- apathy
- increased complaining
- reduced application and lower productivity
- a yearning for yesterday

◆ Staff who have been involved in planning the change or its implementation usually resist less strongly and for a shorter period

Appropriate management responses

During this stage managers should:

◆ Listen and allow resistance and resentment to be expressed rather than bottled up. People like to be able to go home and say "and what's more, I told them so!" They need a safety valve.

◆ Provide the maximum amount of information as a counter to rumor, misinformation (deliberate or otherwise), and anxiety.

◆ Provide information to enable people to engage in change with a sense of purpose or to avoid a situation in which people are without a sense of purpose, regarding the change as a change for its own sake or "for their sake—it does nothing for us."

◆ Seek the views and ideas of staff on implementation of change so that
- staff feel they have a degree of ownership of the change;
- the effectiveness of the implementation is enhanced (staff join in more enthusiastically: two heads are better than one; several are even better).

◆ Recognize that dependency needs become greater.

◆ Be seen by and be close to the staff offering:
  – support
  – reassurance
  – evidence of caring
  – recognition of the contribution of the staff
  – recognition of their needs

Confusion—expected behaviors

◆ There will be some evidence that they "got it off their chests" and of the beginning of acceptance of the change.

◆ Assumption of new roles and development of new relationships will begin.

◆ Indifference and apathy will be replaced by requests for information and clarification, especially about the impact of the change on individuals' jobs.

◆ Negative behavior still includes:
  – fear and confusion as some aspects of the change go well and others do not;
  – fear and confusion as others appear to be adapting to the change more readily;
  – fear of the pace of change, which suggests to some that things may get out of control or at least go beyond their ability to cope.

◆ Positive behavior now includes:
  – seeking clarification of what is expected of the group and of individuals;
  – identification and expression of issues for discussion with management;
  – a preparedness to recognize new opportunities.

Appropriate management responses

During this stage managers should:

◆ Continue to communicate and listen.

◆ Continue to involve staff as much as possible in decisions affecting their work.

◆ State unit/organization objectives so that staff can see where the organization is going, enabling change and its elements to be put into a new perspective.

◆ Explain new work roles and clarify expectations.

◆ Set out functions, responsibilities, and roles.

◆ Restate functions, responsibilities, and roles after an interval to ensure that they have been correctly understood.

◆ Place the highest possible priority on guidance and training, helping staff:
    – to learn new ways of doing things;
    – to form new relationships;
    – to establish new routines;
    – to acquire new knowledge and skills.

◆ Distinguish between attitudes and behavior. Attitudes cannot be changed by edict—negative attitudes can be tolerated if behavior is consistent with the objectives of the change.

◆ Display a clear understanding of the change and commitment to it.

◆ Provide leadership.

Integration—expected behaviors

◆ Optimism begins to replace depression.

◆ Job satisfaction reemerges.

- Anxiety decreases.

- New working relationships become established.

- There is an awareness of behavioral expectations.

- A sense of competence and self-worth returns.

- Staff start looking ahead; thinking progressively ceases to be centered on the past.

Appropriate management responses
During the change managers should:

- Continue to involve the staff in the change process.

- Continue to communicate all possible information and to listen.

Acceptance
We have now reached the situation where:

- Individuals have recovered a sense of self-worth and recovered from any feeling that they were being used to achieve change.

◆ Individuals feel that their contributions are recognized.

◆ Individuals no longer feel threatened.

◆ Working relationships have been reconstructed.

◆ New channels of communication have been established.

◆ Managers can once again distribute their attention between individuals, the team, and the task.

We have a state of relative stability subject only to the impact of other concurrent or expected changes. We should remind ourselves that any special efforts that we have made to communicate more effectively should be perpetuated. Communication is the lubricant of management/staff relationships.

SUMMARY
We have:

◆ Reviewed the psychological impact of change

◆ Looked at the implications of change for human resource management

◆ Considered the four stages of the transitional period

◆ Examined likely staff behavior and appropriate management responses during each stage

Chapter 7

Introducing Change

In this final chapter we are going to look at ways of introducing change, for example, new computer systems, a change that most of us will encounter more than once in our careers.

The topics to be discussed include:

◆ Methods of introducing new systems
  – direct immediate change
  – parallel running
  – pilot projects
  – trial period and review
  – phased or incremental introduction

– change made in successive steps across the whole organization

– total change made in successive parts of the organization

◆ Support during a period of technical change

◆ An action plan for introducing change

METHODS OF INTRODUCING NEW SYSTEMS

Direct immediate change

The old system is discontinued; the new system starts to be used immediately after discontinuation.

Advantages

◆ Clear-cut—less uncertainty overall

◆ Less corporate disruption

◆ Whole organization doing the same thing and uniform standard of service maintained

Disadvantages

◆ Degree of risk—knowledge of acceptability/operation of the new system may be incomplete

◆ Any faults will appear everywhere and cannot be localized

This method of introducing a new system requires prior system testing to be very thorough indeed. It offers no second chance; it must be right the first time.

Parallel running

The existing and new systems operate side by side until satisfaction with the new system enables the old system to be discontinued.

Advantage

◆ There is certainty about the new system before the old system is terminated

Disadvantages

◆ Labor and resource-intensive

◆ Possibility of confusion between old and new systems

This approach ensures continuity of output, but it is only possible to use it if the existing and new systems provide output serving the same purpose.

Pilot projects

This approach uses a pilot project in a discrete part of the organization (often selected because its management is recognized as being pro-change) that is good at coping with change and leading people through it.

Advantage

◆ Facilitation of identification of problems and side-effects not foreseen, without universal disruption

Disadvantage

◆ Uncertainty in sites where pilot projects take place and elsewhere in the organization, probably for different reasons

Those in selected sites know what is happening but are uncertain about its implications for them. Those in other sites may only have a fragmented knowledge of what is happening and may wonder whether they have been excluded for some reason.

Once again we see the importance of timely communication, embracing all those who may be involved or feel concerned.

Pilot sites must be carefully selected with an appropriate typical representation of types of work, caliber of staff, and work pressure.

Trial period and review

This approach is not often used. A minority of activities lend themselves to this approach. The trial is held organization-wide.

Advantages

◆ Avoids commitment to a system that may not work

◆ Shows open-mindedness on the part of management

Disadvantages

◆ Uncertainty during trial period

◆ Uncertainty about period following the trial

Appropriate for highly innovative change when arrangements can be made to protect customers from possible failure of trials.

Phased or incremental introduction

This approach can be subdivided:

1. Whole organization—parts of change introduced sequentially until change is completed.

Advantages

◆ Staff have long periods of adjustment to small steps

◆ Training carried out in steps can be "deeper" and more effective

Disadvantages

◆ Whole procedures become protracted

◆ Some changes/systems do not lend themselves to being broken down

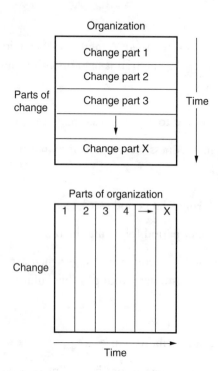

2. Whole change—introduced in successive parts of organization

Advantages

◆ Opportunity to improve as you go

◆ Control over project more easily exercised

Disadvantages

◆ Extended timescale

◆ Problems of selecting order within organization

◆ Some parts feel left out

These approaches may be suitable for very large-scale changes or for geographically dispersed organizations.

SUPPORT DURING A PERIOD OF TECHNICAL CHANGE

Support should be aimed at:

◆ Providing knowledge, skill, and confidence

◆ Enabling staff to cope with change and use the new system effectively and efficiently

◆ Resolving problems and difficulties as they arise

Support may be provided by the department introducing the change (e.g., the computer department).

Whatever arrangements are made to provide support, there is a critical role for managers in providing a two-way communication bridge and in reinforcing the confidence of staff.

Support usually takes the form of a combination of the following:

◆ Training—there will inevitably be scope and need for on-the-job training and coaching whatever overall training arrangements are made.

◆ Manuals and memos—however good these are there will be a need for them to be interpreted and explained, especially to more junior and less experienced staff.

◆ A system support team—may be located centrally or may visit sites as change is introduced. Important role for manager in communicating with support team.

◆ Local support—a skilled user of the existing system who can be particularly useful to the support team in a time of system change.

◆ Managers' support of their staff—counseling, encouraging, and identifying with them.

AN ACTION PLAN FOR INTRODUCING CHANGE

There follows the format of an action plan for introducing change. You may of course need to adapt the format to meet the needs of the project in which you are involved, and you may need more than one copy and more than one version before the project has been completed.

Remember you are not trying to achieve a work of art. Your chosen format is a means to an end, a tool, and not an end in itself. The criterion against which you should judge it is "Is it useful?" and not "Is it artistic?"

ACTION PLAN FOR CHANGE—A USEFUL AND ADAPTABLE FORMAT

NATURE OF CHANGE _____ DATE OF CHANGE _____

Objectives:		Driving forces	Potential resistances	Strategies/actions:			Resource requirements
What?	When?			What?	Who?	When?	

NAME _____ DATE _____ REVIEW DATE _____

95

THE CHANGE PROCESS IN SUMMARY

Here is a handy guide to the main topics covered in this book.

Chapter 1—Understanding change

◆ The nature of change: a framework for understanding change

◆ Some obstacles to managing change effectively

◆ Managers who cope less or more effectively with change

◆ Force field analysis and its use in managing change

Chapter 2—Managing during change

◆ People problems that may arise during change
  - uncertainty and anxiety
  - uncontrolled expectations
  - levels of motivation
  - resistance to change
  - stress
  - role ambiguity
  - hard versus soft management

◆ Dealing with resistance to change
  – knowing your people
  – the role of communication
  – the role of education
  – involvement and participation
  – support by managers
  – selling the advantages of change
  – directing or ordering change

Chapter 6—The psychological impact of change

◆ The transitional period—four stages

◆ Likely behavior and appropriate response during each stage

By this stage you had learned:

◆ You must know people if you are to lead and manage them effectively through change.

◆ You can only know people if you communicate with them on a regular and consistent basis.

Chapter 7—Introducing change

◆ Methods of introducing new systems
  – direct immediate change
  – parallel running
  – pilot projects
  – trial period and review
  – phased or incremental introduction (i.e., change made in successive steps across the whole organization or total change made in successive parts of the organization)

◆ Support during a period of technical change

INDEX